Help Yourself to God's Help

Travis Monday

Help Yourself to God's Help

By Travis Monday

ISBN 978-0-6151-4077-3

Copyright 2007 by Travis Monday

Online editions may also be available for this title. For more information, please visit www.lulu.com.

All rights reserved. No part of this book may be reproduced or transmitted in any form or by any means without permission by the author.

"Scripture quotations marked (HCSB) are taken from the Holman Christian Standard Bible®, Copyright © 1999, 2000, 2002, 2003 by Holman Bible Publishers. Used by permission. Holman Christian Standard Bible®, Holman CSB®, and HCSB® are federally registered trademarks of Holman Bible Publishers."

"Scripture quotations marked (NASB) are taken from the New American Standard Bible®, Copyright © 1960, 1962, 1963, 1968, 1971, 1972, 1973, 1975, 1977, 1995 by The Lockman Foundation Used by permission." (www.Lockman.org)

"Scripture quotations marked (NKJV) are taken from the New King James Version. Copyright © 1982 by Thomas Nelson, Inc. Used by permission. All rights reserved."

"Scripture quotations marked (NLT) are taken from the *Holy Bible*, New Living Translation, copyright © 1996. Used by permission of Tyndale House Publishers, Inc., Wheaton, Illinois 60189. All rights reserved."

Printed in the United States of America

Dedication

This book is dedicated to my brother, Derrell Monday, in appreciation for his prayers and for his other efforts to help point me in the right direction.

Acknowledgments

I owe a debt of gratitude to a good number of people who helped me with this book by answering and returning to me a questionnaire. The following people helped me in this way: Ron Bruton, Milton Tyler, Lenard A. Hartley, Clara Rinehart, M. B. Weaver, Donna Riddle, Penny Hogue, Helen Nixon, Doris Walker Bullock, Colleen Heath, Mary Robbins, and Beta Little. Thank you, my friends, for your assistance with this project.

Table of Contents

Introduction 1

Why Do I Need God's Help? 5

Does God Really Want to Help Me? 11

What Kind of Help Does God Give? 15

When Will God Help Me? 23

How Will God Help Me? 29

How Can I Help Myself to God's Help? 37

Will God's Help Make Me Happy? 51

How Can I Help Others Get God's Help? 59

Can I Help God? 63

Bibliography 69

Introduction

"God helps those who help themselves." You've heard it and so have I. Doesn't it *sound* true? Doesn't it even *feel* true?

After many years of hearing that statement, I began hearing it challenged. "God helps those who realize that they can't help themselves." In some ways that sounds and feels true also.

So, which statement should we believe?

Before I answer that question, let me say that both of these statements have strengths and weaknesses, and both relate to the ongoing obsession of Americans with self-help.

Self-Help Society

Why describe American culture as a self-help society?

Consider our saturation with self-help literature. Take a trip down to any mainstream American bookstore and you'll see what I mean. Self-help books sell quite well in the United States and they've done so many years. But are they actually helping anyone?

Tom Tiede, author of *Self-Help Nation*, doesn't think so. He even compares the writers of self-help books to the peddlers of snake oil from an earlier time in our history. And in some cases, he may be right, but not always. He trashes self-help books of both the religious and non-religious varieties.

Self-Help Versus God's Help

The topic of self-help and self-help literature prompts us to ask, "Is self-help enough?"

> *Self-help isn't enough.*

From the title of this book you've already figured out that I believe the answer is "no." Self-help isn't enough, and I'll say more about that later.

Self-Help Extremes

Now, let's return to those two earlier statements about whom God helps. They capture the essence of how we have approached the idea of accessing God's help throughout the history of our nation, and they can, depending on how they are used, also represent two extremes in how we think about getting God's help.

First, let's consider the statement: "God helps those who help themselves." Many people like this statement and we might even say that it embodies our belief in self-reliance – a belief particularly attractive to Americans.

"God helps those who help themselves." These words ring true for many people because they remind us of the need to accept personal responsibility, that is, responsibility for how we respond to both problems and opportunities.

Unfortunately, these same words, carried to the extreme, may push us toward excessive self-reliance rather than reliance upon God. We face the danger of focusing too much on the words "help themselves" and too little on the words, "God helps."

Next, let's consider the statement: "God helps those who realize that they can't help themselves." Because of the danger of relying upon ourselves rather than upon God, some people have turned to this statement in place of "God helps those who help themselves."

Once again, we have a statement with both strengths and weaknesses. Saying, "God helps those who realize that they can't help themselves," helps us by pushing us toward a much-needed reliance upon God. But, when carried to the extreme, these words can become an excuse for ignoring our responsibility to do something about our problems.

A New Way of Saying What We May Already Know

What we say matters and how we say it matters, so I'm always working to find better ways to share truth. After years of struggling over how to talk about getting God's help, I came up with an alternative approach, that is, a different way to talk about accessing God's help.

Instead of saying, "God helps those who help themselves," or "God helps those who realize that they can't help themselves," I prefer to say, "God helps those who help themselves to His help."

I've eaten in many homes where one of the hosts would say something like this: "There's plenty of food for everyone, but around here you've got to learn to help yourself. If you don't get enough to eat, it's your own fault." Likewise, God has generously made His help available to us, but we need to learn to help ourselves to it.

Notice that this statement, by referring to God's help twice, reinforces the emphasis on our need for His help. It also maintains the idea that we need to accept our responsibility to take advantage of His help.

God helps those who help themselves to His help.

Nine Key Questions Related to God's Help

After I spoke to a crowd on the topic of getting God's help, a lady approached me and said, "I want to help myself to God's help." I'm convinced that many other people want the same thing.

In order to help ourselves to God's help, we need think our way through this topic, and asking the right questions can aid us in this process. For that reason I've built this book around nine key questions:

1. Why do I need God's help?
2. Does God really want to help me?
3. What kind of help does God give?
4. When will God help me?
5. How will God help me?
6. How can I help myself to God's help?
7. Will God's help make me happy?
8. How can I help others get God's help?
9. Can I help God?

As we prepare to engage our heads and our hearts in seeking to find God's help for ourselves and others, I close with this basic truth: *God invites you to help yourself to His help.*

Why Do I Need God's Help?

> In this time I have had cancer, I have tried
> to have a positive attitude. If I can't
> trust God for His help, I have no hope.
>
> --Penny Hogue

Perhaps you've heard the old expression, "Lord knows the trouble I've seen." Maybe you've even spoken those words yourself. You may wonder how you can possibly overcome the overwhelming problems that have invaded your life.

God's Help – Our Hope

Trouble assaults all of us, but God can help us triumph over trouble. Jesus said, "These things I have spoken to you, that in Me you may have peace. In the world you have tribulation, but take courage; I have overcome the world."[1]

> *Since Jesus overcame the world, He can help us overcome our problems.*

Since Jesus overcame the world, He can help us overcome our problems. Through faith in Jesus Christ, the same Jesus who died on a cross and rose from the grave, God's help becomes our hope. Without God's

---

[1] John 16:33, NASB.

help, we have little if any reason for hope, but with His help hope can fill our lives and overflow into the lives of others.

Reasons We Need God's Help

You may have already spotted some of the reasons why we need God's help from what I've already said, but let's dig deeper by considering a list of reasons.

Life is hard and trouble surrounds us.

To live is to know trouble and hardship. The words of Penny Hogue cited at the beginning of this chapter point out one type of hardship – declining health. Penny wrote those words while facing cancer. People of all ages face physical health problems, and as we age, we reach a point where we can sense that we are losing ground physically.

While writing this book, I underwent hernia surgery for the second time. Years earlier, I had the same surgery and bounced back quickly, and even returned to work that same week. But this time that didn't happen. My body doesn't heal as fast as in the past. Then the following month, I entered a local hospital through the Emergency Room suffering from severe pain. A short time later, surgeons removed my gall bladder. Physically speaking, I'm losing ground, and that fact reminds me of my need for God.

> *The hardness of life can help us recognize our need for God's help.*

Of course, declining health is only one of the many types of trouble we encounter in this life. We face family problems, financial worries, legal entanglements, unjust criticism, career setbacks, the death of loved ones, and others.

Why Do I Need God's Help?

The hardness of life can help us recognize our need for God's help. It is not enough to simply say, "When the going gets tough, the tough get going." Instead, we need to help ourselves to God's help, so let's consider another reason why we need His help.

None of us always gets it right.

We all mess up from time to time whether we admit it or not. Sometimes we blow it. In other words, we need God because of weaknesses within ourselves.

Our failure to always get it right includes moral mess-ups. Of all the ways we can blow it, messing up morally is the worst. We don't get it right morally speaking when we put our ways above God's ways, yet all of us have that tendency.

> *We need God because of weaknesses within ourselves.*

When we get old enough to start choosing between right and wrong, we tend to make choices that displease the God who created us.

The only one who *always* gets it right is God, so we all need His help. We also need God's help for another reason.

God created us to need Him and know Him.

God created the heavens and the earth and all of life, and that includes the human race. When He created people, He made them in His image so that they could have a personal relationship with Him that would last forever.

Can you imagine that? The same God who created the universe designed us to have a personal relationship with Him! Through that relationship we can experience a wonderful fulfillment in life that we cannot experience in any other way.

God created us with a built-in need for Him that we cannot afford to ignore. If we reject God's offer of a relationship with Him, we cut ourselves off from much of the help He wants to give us.

My wife and I have two sons. If they cut themselves off from us and refuse to listen to us, we cannot help them as much as we want. By neglecting their relationship with us they miss out on what we have to offer them. Likewise, we cannot help ourselves to God's help without entering into a personal relationship with Him. After we enter into a relationship with God through faith in Jesus Christ, we then need to nurture and cultivate that relationship.

Without God we cannot possibly fulfill our potential.

In creating us for a special relationship with Him, God also created us with tremendous potential. He wants to help us fulfill that potential. God wants to help us be all that we can be both now and in the future – a future that stretches throughout the rest of eternity.

> *Many people never fulfill their potential because they choose to leave God out of their lives.*

Unfortunately, many people never fulfill their potential because they choose to leave God out of their lives. But it doesn't have to be that way. When you ignore God, you sabotage your future and miss your potential. You can't' help yourself to God's help by doing that!

Only God can completely forgive our moral mess-ups.

During my college days at Hardin-Simmons University in Abilene, Texas, I spent some time as a member of First Baptist Church. In fact, I met my future wife there at a social event for college students.

Why Do I Need God's Help?

Dr. James Flaming, the pastor, talked one day about a popular book called, *I'm OK – You're OK*, by Thomas A. Harris.[2] In response to that title Flaming said, "I'm *not* OK – you're *not* OK, but in Christ that's OK." God makes it OK by forgiving us for our wrongdoing.

> *We all need to help ourselves to God's help by helping ourselves to His forgiveness.*

Since we all blow it, morally speaking, by putting our ways above God's ways, we all need God's forgiveness. None of us can afford to walk through life without it. We all need to help ourselves to God's help by helping ourselves to His forgiveness.

> If there were only records, Lord,
> of all I've said and done;
> If there were only records, Lord,
> I'd be a doomed man.
>
> But forgiveness was, forgiveness is,
> and forgiveness will always be,
> Your shredding machine for records of sin –
> Your Christ-kept file on me.[3]

---

[2] Thomas A. Harris, *I'm OK – You're Ok* (New York: Avon Books, 1973).

[3] Travis Monday, "Just for the Record" in *Poems of Faith for People of Faith* (United States of America: Lulu Press, 2006), 22.

Only God can give us eternal life.

The Bible speaks of a special kind of life known as eternal life. Along with lasting forever, eternal life includes a better quality of life in the here and now. Any other approach to life means settling for less than the best – God's best.

This idea of eternal life takes us back to the idea of a personal relationship with God. Jesus described eternal life as a relationship when He prayed, "And this is eternal life, that they may know Thee, the only true God, and Jesus Christ whom Thou has sent."[4]

We Need God's Help

This list of reasons of why we need God's help could easily be enlarged, but I've made my point: *We all need God's help.*

Whether or not you agree with my conclusion, I urge you to keep reading. God may use something in the remainder of this book to help awaken you to your need for Him.

---

[4] John 17:3, NASB.

Does God Really Want to Help Me?

> And we have come to know and to
> believe the love that God has for us.
>
> --1 John 4:16a, HCSB

Who Cares If I Need Help?

Does anyone really care about your needs? Most of us can think of at least a few people who care about us, and who, therefore, would want to help us with our problems. We do well to thank God for such people.

What about the government? Does the government care about your problems and mine? Government itself cannot care about anyone or anything since it is not a person, but perhaps some people in the government care about people. Of course, some people in government care more about their own careers and interests than about you and me.

And what about religion? Do religious people reflect a genuine concern for our needs? Sometimes. But in many cases they tend to care more about values, laws, and belief systems than about individuals – even if those values, laws, or belief systems claim to value individuals.

So, does anyone really care if we need help? The title of this book, *Help Yourself to God's Help*, correctly implies that *God cares about us*.

God Cares About You and Your Needs

> But God proves His own love
> for us in that while we were
> yet sinners Christ died for us!
>
> --Romans 5:8, HCSB

Even though we don't always get it right, God loves us so much that He let His son, Jesus Christ, die on a cross for us. Jesus did not die for His own moral mess-ups – He had none; He died for ours. Jesus, unlike us, always gets it right, but He willingly gave His life for those who don't, and that includes you and me.

> *Jesus did not die for His own moral mess-ups – He had none; He died for ours.*

Jesus himself once said, "Greater love has no one than this, that one lay down his life for his friends."[1] And that's what Jesus did for us when He died on a cross.

As Philip Yancey explains in his book, *Disappointment with God*: "At once, the Cross revealed what kind of world we have and what kind of God we have: a world of gross unfairness, a God of sacrificial love."[2]

God cares about you as an individual.

> Give all your worries and cares to God,
> for he cares about what happens to you.
> --1 Peter 5:7, NLT

---

[1] John 15:13, NASB.

[2] Philip Yancey, *Disappointment with God* (Grand Rapids, Michigan: Zondervan Publishing House, 1988), 186.

Jeremiah lived in the days of the Bible's Old Testament. He eventually served God as a preacher or prophet. Some Bible commentators like to call to him "The Weeping Prophet" because he wept for his people when they refused to stop putting their ways above God's ways.

Shortly before Jeremiah started preaching, God said to him, "Before I formed you in the womb I knew you."[3] Do you get it? God knew Jeremiah as an individual even before Jeremiah's birth!

God cannot care about you individually unless He first knows you as an individual. He knew Jeremiah and He knows you.

After indicating that not even one sparrow could fall to the ground without God knowing about it, Jesus said, "And the very hairs on your head are all numbered. So don't be afraid; you are more valuable to him than a whole flock of sparrows."[4]

> *God knows you and everything about you whether you know Him or not.*

God knows you and everything about you whether you know Him or not. To Him you are not just a Social Security number or a mere drop lost in the vast sea of humanity.

God loves you and wants to meet your needs.

> Since God did not spare even his own Son but gave him up for us all, won't God, who gave us Christ, also give us everything else?
> --Romans 8:32, NLT

---

[3] Jeremiah 1:5a, NKJV.

[4] Matthew 10:30-31, NLT.

> And my God will supply all your needs
> according to His riches in glory in Christ Jesus.
>
> --Phil 4:19, HCSB

One of my teachers, Oscar Thompson, defined love in a simple yet profound way. He said, "Love is meeting needs."[5] When God proved His love for us by giving His son, Jesus Christ, to die for us, He did so in order to meet our needs. God knew we needed someone special to help us enter into a personal relationship with Him, and Jesus Christ does that for us when we invite Him into our lives. God really does want to help you and that's why He sent Jesus.

So, helping ourselves to God's help means helping ourselves to God's love. And we can help ourselves to God's love by letting Him meet our needs.

By the way, our greatest need is for God.

> *God really does want to help you and that's why He sent Jesus.*

---

[5] W. Oscar Thompson, Jr., *Concentric Circles of Concern* (Nashville, Tennessee: Broadman Press, 1981), 33.

What Kind of Help Does God Give?

> O taste and see that the LORD is good;
> How blessed is the man who takes refuge in Him!
>
> --Psalm 34:8, NASB

My wife and I, like a lot of other people, love to eat out. And when we find a restaurant with exceptionally good-tasting food, we tend to go there every chance we get. Every time we go back to that restaurant, we expect to get food of the highest quality.

When we help ourselves to God's help, what kind of help can we expect? *God offers us the best possible help.*

But let me clarify where I'm going with this chapter. I'm not talking about the *forms* God's help takes, we will look at that later, but rather the focus is on the *quality* of God's help.

> *God offers us the best possible help.*

When you discover how much better God's help is compared to other sources of help, you will never be satisfied with anything else.

Why should we want God's help rather than the alternatives that the world throws at us? Let's consider a few reasons found in the Bible in Psalm 121. In addition we will consider other Scriptures from the Bible that also talk about God's help.

God offers us powerful help.

> My help comes from the Lord,
> Who made heaven and earth.
>
> --Psalm 121:2, NASB

The psalmist reminds us that God is the Creator of the universe. This image of God as Creator presents Him as capable of giving us powerful help. *Only a great and powerful God could have created the heavens and the earth.*

You might want to ask yourself whether you have a big God or a little God. A little girl listened attentively as her father read the family devotions. She seemed awed by her parents' talk of God's limitless power and mercy.

"Daddy," she asked, placing her little hands on his knees, "how big is God?" Her father thought for a moment and answered, "Honey, He is always just a little bigger then you need."

Although I like that story, I take issue with the part about God being "just a *little* bigger than you need." God always is *much* bigger than you need. His power exceeds anything we can imagine.

The same God who created the universe is powerful enough to help us with our problems. David, one of Israel's greatest kings, understood this when he wrote, "The Lord is my strength and my shield; my heart trusts in Him, and I am helped."[1]

> *The same God who created the universe is powerful enough to help us with our problems.*

---

[1] Psalm 28:7, NASB.

So, the real question is not: How big are my problems? Instead, we need to ask: How big is my God?

You can't help yourself to God's help by making your problems bigger than God. See Him as He is – powerful enough to give you the help you need.

God offers us perceptive help.

Without question God knows what He is doing. The writer of Psalm 121 presents God as perceptive enough to know how to keep our feet from slipping as we travel the dangerous paths of life.

God knows how to guide our feet and keep them from slipping because He is all-knowing. Nothing is hidden from God.

> *God knows what He is doing.*

Suppose you had to cross a field full of deadly land mines. One wrong step and you get blown up. Also suppose that a person who knew exactly where every one of the mines was buried offered to take you through it. Would you say to him, "I don't want you to tell me what to do. I don't want you to impose your ways on me. I'll just cross this mine field my way."?

I can't speak for you, but I would gladly accept the help of such a person. I'd want to stay as close to him as I could instead of wandering off into a deadly mine field on my own. His directions could save my life. He would say, "Don't go that way because it will kill you. Don't step there if you want to avoid getting blown up. Go this way, instead, and you will live."

Likewise, God's commands grow out of life-saving insight. He knows what we need and He knows the best ways to meet our needs.

When God gives you a command, He is trying to protect and preserve you. He does not want you to step on a mine or slip into a booby-trapped pit. Instead of viewing God's commands as restricting you, understand that He is freeing you from dangers and distractions so that you can fulfill your potential.

> *God's commands grow out of life-saving insight.*

While still a child growing up in West Texas, I often watched a television show called "Father Knows Best." Now, at a time when I'm about to enter the senior adult stage of life, I say with confidence that God the Father knows best. He gives you *perceptive* help because He knows what is best for you.

> *God gives you perceptive help because He knows what is best for you.*

Another reason God's help is perceptive is that God never falls asleep on duty; He stays alert and aware of the dangers that surround us.

While serving in the U.S. Army, I sometimes struggled to stay awake and alert on guard duty. Like an enemy soldier, sleep would sneak up on me and try to "put me out of action."

Sleep cannot sneak up on God. As the psalmist put it, "He who keeps you will not slumber."[2] In other words, you will never catch God sleeping on the job. His unending alertness and unequalled awareness enable Him

---

[2] Psalm 121:3b, NASB.

to see the dangers that threaten us. With His help we can overcome them.

Doesn't it make sense to trust in a God who knows *You will never catch God sleeping on the job.* exactly what we need and exactly when we need it? And doesn't it make sense to seek help from a God who knows where we need to go and how to best get us there?

God offers us protective help.

The Bible presents God as one who protects us day and night from both physical and spiritual dangers. Although we are not guaranteed that we will never be physically harmed in any way, we can know that God will provide us with the protection we need to fulfill His plan and purpose for our lives.

As the psalmist declared, "He will protect you from all evil; He will keep your soul."[3]

David believed in helping himself to God's help. He described God as a protective shield, saying, "The LORD is my strength and my shield; my heart trusts in Him, and I am helped."[4]

In another passage David spoke of God as "a shield about me."[5] The modern equivalent to a shield in science fiction is a force field consisting

---

[3] Psalm 121:7, NASB.

[4] Psalm 28:7a, NASB.

[5] Psalm 3:3, NASB.

of a barrier of invisible energy surrounding a space ship. When we help ourselves to God's help, the Lord surrounds us with a "force field" of His protective presence. A more contemporary version of this verse might read, "But You, O Lord, are a force field around me."

We all know that a shield is useless unless used. During the war in Vietnam soldiers received flak jackets designed to help protect them from fragments from grenades, artillery rounds, rockets, and mortars. Sometimes soldiers chose not to wear their flak jackets and suffered serious injury or even death that the flak jackets might have prevented. Likewise, unless we help ourselves to God's protective help, we may suffer injuries of various sorts that God could have prevented. In other words, God does not force us to help ourselves to His help.

> *God does not force us to help ourselves to His help.*

One word of caution – when we refer to God as a shield we should guard against thinking of Him as an "it" rather than as a living being with whom we can enjoy a personal relationship. I don't mind if my wife thinks of me as a shield or protector, but I also want her to think of me as a person who knows her personally. God knows us personally and desires to protect us from danger.

God offers us permanent help.

Temporary help agencies specialize in providing employers with temporary workers. Those agencies can provide good sources of *temporary* help. But when we go to God for help we can expect Him to offer us more than temporary help; God offers *permanent* help. He doesn't start to help us then bail out when the going gets tough. He sticks with us to the end.

"The Lord will guard your going out and your coming in."[6] In other words, God will protect us. But the rest of that same verse asserts that *God never stops guarding us.* The psalmist says that God guards our going out and our coming in "From this time forth and forever."[7]

Why does the Lord offer us permanent help? Because He loves us and because His love for us will never end. As the psalmist wrote: "The Lord will work out his plans for my life – for your faithful love, O Lord, endures forever."[8]

> *God's love for us will never end.*

---

[6] Psalm 121:8a, NASB.

[7] Psalm 121:8b, NASB.

[8] Psalm 138:8, NLT.

When Will God Help Me?

> That guy is late for everything! He will
> probably be late for his own funeral!
>
> --Popular saying

A Man Who Was Late for His Own Funeral

Sometimes people will say about someone who is habitually late, "He will probably be late for his own funeral." In Colorado City in Mitchell County, Texas, one of their most famous citizens really was late for his own funeral.

By the time he resigned from the Texas Rangers to become the first sheriff of Mitchell County, Richard Clayton (Dick) Ware had already become famous for his part in the shoot-out with the notorious Sam Bass and his gang in Round Rock, Texas. After a decade of service as Mitchell County's sheriff, Ware received an appointment as the U. S. Marshal for the Western District of Texas.

When Ware died in a Fort Worth hospital on June 25, 1902, plans were made for his funeral and burial in Colorado City. Although planned for earlier in the day, his funeral had to be delayed until 5:00 p.m. because Ware's body did not arrive soon enough to have the funeral at the scheduled time. According to a story in *West Texas Stockman*, the train carrying

Ware's body "was six hours late," so Dick Ware really was late for his own funeral.[1]

Although you and I may never be late for our own funeral, most of us are late many times during our lives, but God never shows up late for anything!

> *God never shows up late for anything!*

Don't Be Late – Help Yourself to God's Help Right Now

Our addiction to the gospel of self-reliance may cause us to view God as a last resort. When all else fails, we finally turn to Him. That makes us habitually late to help ourselves to God's help.

When and Willingness

> A few weeks ago I gave God a burden I had carried for thirty years. I was home and alone, and it just came to me: "I cannot carry this burden any longer." So I said, "Lord, I give You this burden." Immediately, it was gone. I felt as if a physical load had been removed from my shoulders and mind. A great peace came into my heart as God said to me, "Don't you think I can take care of this?"
>
> --Mary Robbins

---

[1] *West Texas Stockman*, 1 July 1902, p. 1.

These words from Mary Robbins, a faithful member of a church I served as pastor, help us see how we can be late about helping ourselves to God's help. We may even unintentionally carry a burden that God wants us to give to Him. Fortunately for us, we can recognize what we've been doing and change our tactics.

But sometimes we may give a burden to the Lord only to take it back and carry it around again. I've lost count of the times that I've done that. This tendency points to our need to learn to help ourselves to God's help *everyday*.

When and Waiting

> O God, don't stay away. My
> God, please hurry to help me.
>
> --Psalm 71:12, NLT

> But those who wait upon God get fresh
> strength. They will fly high on wings
> like eagles. They will run and not grow
> weary. They will walk and not faint.
>
> --Isaiah 40:31, NLT

When you've felt a need for God's help, perhaps you've thought or said, "I want God's help *right now!*" We never want to wait for God's help. Like the writer of Psalm 71, we want God to "please hurry" to help us.

> *Like it or not, sometimes God makes us wait.*

The words quoted above from Isaiah 40:31 assure us of God's help, but they also tell us that we may have to wait a while. Like it or not, sometimes God makes us wait.

> *Sometimes helping ourselves to God's help means letting Him teach us how to wait on Him.*

Sometimes helping ourselves to God's help means letting Him teach us how to wait on Him. And God is quite willing to start teaching us how to wait on Him as soon as we turn to Him for help. And sometimes we wait when we don't have to wait; we simply fail to help ourselves to God's help.

When will God help us? To some degree *when* God helps us depends on our willingness to let Him help us. As we become willing, *when* gets closer.

> *Sometimes we wait when we don't have to; we simply fail to help ourselves to God's help.*

When will God help us? He will help us right now even if that means helping us to wait on Him for some other type of help.

Waiting on God may include waiting for results in our efforts to make this world a better place. The Bible says, "So don't get tired of doing what is good. Don't get discouraged and give up, for we will reap a harvest of blessing at the appropriate time."[2]

---

[2] Galatians 6:9, NLT.

God will help us right now even if helping us right now means helping us to wait for His timing. Waiting for God's timing requires patience, but God can help us with that, too. And God may use waiting to help us mature. As Richard Hendrix explains, "Second only to suffering, waiting may be the greatest teacher and trainer in godliness, maturity, and genuine spirituality most of us ever encounter."[3]

> *When will God help us? He will help us right now even if that means helping us to wait on Him for some other type of help.*

When and the Will of God

> Daily I call on my Lord . . .
> for help to make another day.
>
> --Colleen Heath

I admit it – knowing God's will can prove difficult at times, but that shouldn't surprise us when we understand that God's thoughts are higher than our thoughts and God's ways are higher than our ways.[4]

Colleen Heath, like some other people I know, has learned the wisdom of asking the Lord for strength and guidance every day. This one-day-at-

---

[3] Richard Hendrix, *Leadership*, Vol. 7, No. 3.

[4] See Isaiah 55:9.

a-time approach to discovering God's will and receiving His help makes sense because we might not have a tomorrow.

Although we can and even should make plans for the future, those plans may or may not work out, and God's timing may not fit our schedules.

Regardless of how we view God's timing, the Bible teaches that God not only knows *what* we need but *when* we need it. We can trust God's timing even when we want to question it.

> *We can trust God's timing even when we want to question it.*

How Will God Help Me?

Complicated — that's a good word for describing life in today's world. A cowboy I knew who worked on a Texas ranch told me that he should have been born during the 1800's when life was simpler. He felt unsuited for the complexities of modern life, and sometimes we feel the same way.

Nothing seems simple anymore. Rules, regulations, and paperwork bombard us. Simple tasks turn into difficult time-consuming undertakings that threaten to take us under. They leave us feeling frustrated and fed up.

The confusing nature of life in a complicated world can actually help us recognize our need for God, and that's a good thing. But sometimes the ways of God confuse us and make it harder to recognize the success of our efforts to help ourselves to God's help.

> *The confusing nature of life in a complicated world can actually help us recognize our need for God, and that's a good thing.*

Because of who God is and because of our human limitations, we sometimes fail to recognize God's help when He gives it. When we do recognize it, we may struggle to understand it.

Yet, God's will is always best — even when we don't understand it fully, even when we question and doubt, and even when we wish God would do things differently.

Help Yourself to God's Help

Since God can help us in many different ways, this chapter is about watching God work so we can discover *how* He works and *how* He helps us.

God Works

> From one man He made every nation of
> men to live all over the earth and has determined
> their appointed times and the boundaries of
> where they live, so that they might seek God,
> and perhaps they might reach out and find Him,
> though He is not far from each of us.
>
> --Acts 17:26-27, HCSB

God works all the time and He wants to work in our behalf. He has His hands on human history and offers Himself to us no matter when we live or where we live. When we put our lives in His hands, He causes all things to work together for our good.

God works by being at the right place at the right time. He is a very present help in times of trouble. God even promises never to forsake or abandon us. In other words, He works through His presence.

> *God works by being at the right place at the right time.*

God is here and God is there and God is everywhere doing His work. He wants us to recognize both His activity and His presence and to maintain that awareness. As someone once said, "To see God's hand in everything makes life a great adventure."[1]

---

[1] *Our Daily Bread.* Ed. Tom Gustafon. Vol. 51, No. 9, 10 & 11. December 2006, January & February 2007.

God Works Through His Word

> So My word that comes from My
> mouth will not return to Me empty,
> but will accomplish what I please, and
> will prosper in what I send it [to do].
>
> --Isaiah 55:13, HCSB

In the past God worked through men inspired by His Spirit to produce His Word – the Bible. A God capable of creating and sustaining the universe certainly can produce an effective manual for life for the people He made. As Paul the Apostle declared, "All Scripture is inspired by God and is useful to teach us what is true and to make us realize what is wrong in our lives. It corrects us when we are wrong and teaches us to do what is right. God uses it to prepare and equip his people to do every good work."[2] God's Word works and God works through His Word, so we can expect Him to help us through the truths of Scripture.

> *God's Word works and God works through His Word.*

God Works *in* People.

> And I am sure that God, who began
> the good work within you, will continue
> his work until it is finally finished on that
> day when Christ Jesus comes back again.
>
> --Philippians 1:6, NLT

---

[2] 2 Timothy 3:16-17, NLT.

> I need to let God be God
> and let Him be in control.
>
> --Donna Riddle

God wants to begin a good work in you. If you have trusted in Jesus Christ as your Lord and Savior, He has already begun a good work in you. If you have not yet asked Jesus to be your personal Lord and Savior, then He is waiting for your invitation so that He can get started on the good work He wants to do in you.

> *Fortunately for us, the Lord Jesus Christ can finish what He starts, and that includes the good work He begins in us.*

Fortunately for us, the Lord Jesus Christ can finish what He starts, and that includes the good work He begins in us. Our Lord can bring that good work to completion.

For us to get the best benefit of the Lord's work in us, we need to surrender control of our lives to Him everyday. That's what it means for Him to be our "Lord." God wants to do His good work in us, and when we let Him do His work in us, we are helping ourselves to His help.

> *God wants to do His good work in us, and when we let Him do His work in us, we are helping ourselves to His help.*

God Works *Through* People.

If God can work *in* me, He also can work *through* me. And if God can work through me, He can work through you. And if He can work through you and me, then He can work through others. Because God works through people, we need to pay attention to what He is doing in and through the lives of the people around us. He may choose to help us through some of those people.

God works in us and through us when we help ourselves to His help. And understand this: God does not work only through perfect

> *God works in us and through us when we help ourselves to His help.*

people. Only Jesus Christ lived a perfect life. Because of His amazing grace, God works in and through imperfect people in an imperfect world.

God Works *by* His Spirit.

> I try to trust God to lead in every undertaking.
> This means a cultivation of a mentality of
> trusting Him to lead me day by day,
> step by step, and moment by moment.
>
> --Helen Nixon
>
> I must be ready, attuned, and
> aware when the Holy Spirit is
> guiding, nudging, and helping me.
>
> --Beta Little

> *God's Spirit provides God's help day by day, step by step, and moment by moment.*

All believers in the Lord Jesus Christ have access to God's counsel from the Holy Spirit, who is the presence of God in us. God's Spirit provides God's help. God's Spirit provides God's help day by day, step by step, and moment by moment.

Jesus spoke of the Holy Spirit when He said, "And I will ask the Father and He will give you another Counselor to be with you forever. He is the

Spirit of truth."[3] The word **Counselor** in this verse may also be translated "Comforter" or "Helper." When we help ourselves to God's Spirit, we are helping ourselves to God's help. God works in and through us by the Holy Spirit.

By the way, when we help ourselves to God's Spirit, the Spirit of God helps us become more like Jesus Christ.

God Works *In* and *Through* Circumstances

> And we know that God causes everything to work
> together for the good of those who love God
> and are called according to his purpose for them.
>
> --Romans 8:28, NLT

God has His hand in human history, and that includes the daily activities of our lives. And God works through both positive and negative events and circumstances.

No matter what we think about the events unfolding before us, we need to keep watching for God's hand in human history. And whether or not we can figure out what God is up to in a particular situation, we need to keep on helping ourselves to His help.

When we develop a lifestyle of helping ourselves to God's help, we will see God working in our own lives and in the lives of others. We will also develop an ability to recognize His work in and through circumstances of every kind. And we will begin to understand that He loves us more than

---

[3] John 14:16-17a, HCSB.

we can even start to imagine. Eventually we will know that God's work, at some level and in some way, is always an expression of His everlasting love, and His love makes life better.

> The painful moments
> of our journey on earth
> cause us to question
> and doubt life's worth.
> Then Jesus comes
> in His glory and grace,
> and makes this world
> a far better place.[4]

---

[4] Travis Monday, "Relief" in *Poems of Faith for People of Faith* (United States of America: Lulu Press, 2006), 2.

How Can I Help Myself to God's Help?

> Believing in God and trusting in
> Him is the best thing we can do.
>
> --Penny Hogue

Penny Hogue wrote, "Believing in God and trusting in Him is the best thing we can do," while fighting cancer – for the second time! As her pastor I had especially wanted her input for this book because I could sense the strength of her faith in God. I found in her an example of someone helping herself to God's help, and watching her walk with God inspired me and others to trust in the Lord through thick and thin.

Trusting in the Lord in all circumstances enables us to help ourselves to His help, so I'll mention faith repeatedly throughout this chapter while listing and explaining various aspects of living by faith.

One of the most popular approaches to self-help books is the how-to book.

> *Trusting in the Lord in all circumstances enables us to help ourselves to His help.*

Many of these books include the words "how to" in the title. For example, I have a book in my personal library called *How to Deal with How You Feel*, by Ralph Speas.

Dr. W. E. (Bill) Thorn, a member of Immanuel Baptist Church in San Angelo, Texas, is a noted preacher, teacher, and humorist who has written many books. In the preface to his book, *Dairy Queen "Think Tank,"* he says, "I have discovered the secret of writing a successful book. If you write a book entitled, *How to Fail*, and it fails, it is a success."[1] I'm grateful that the Lord blesses us with people who can help us laugh – especially at ourselves.

Let's consider some how-to principles related to helping ourselves to God's help.

Admitting My Need for God's Help

> I know I can help myself to God's help by acknowledging my weaknesses and limitations.
>
> --Clara Rinehart

How can we help ourselves to God's help? One way is to admit that we need His help. Many people never admit their need for God, and therefore they don't experience Him as a very present help in times of trouble.

> *Many people never admit their need for God, and therefore they don't experience Him as a very present help in times of trouble.*

---

[1] W. E. Thorn, *Dairy Queen "Think Tank"* (Fayetteville, North Carolina: Old Mountain Press, 2002), vii.

Faith in God includes an honest admission of our need for God. And we don't just *sort of* need God; we need Him *desperately*. We need to reject the self-help philosophy that says, "I can do just fine without God." Instead, we need to agree with Jesus Christ when He

> *We need to reject the self-help philosophy that says, "I can do just fine without God."*

says, "For apart from Me you can do nothing."[2] In the last chapter of this book, I'll emphasize this truth again because I cannot overstate its importance.

Asking God for His Help

> I just need to ask Him for it.
>
> --Donna Riddle
>
> I would first ask if they had a daily prayer relationship with God.
>
> --Ron Bruton
>
> First a person has to pray.
>
> --M. B. Weaver
>
> I called to the Lord in my distress,
> and I cried to my God for help.
> From His temple He heard my voice,
> and my cry to Him reached His ears.
>
> --Psalm 18:6, HCSB

---

[2] John 15:5, NASB.

"How can I help myself to God's help?" When I asked a group of men how they would answer this question, one of them said, "Ask – ask God for His help." According to Jesus Christ, that's an excellent answer!

We help ourselves to God's help by asking, seeking, and knocking. Jesus said, "Keep asking, and it will be given to you. Keep searching, and you will find. Keep knocking, and the door will be opened to you. For everyone who asks receives, and the one who searches finds, and to the one who knocks, the door will be opened."[3]

> *We help ourselves to God's help by asking, seeking, and knocking.*

When we ask God for help, we are praying, so prayer is one of the ways that we help ourselves to God's help.

Accepting the Help God Offers

Since God doesn't force Himself or His ways on us, we need to accept His help in order to get it. So let's consider a couple of the primary ways we can accept God's help.

You see, we can help ourselves to God's help by . . .

Accepting Jesus Christ as Savior and Lord

> First, establish a relationship with God by
> accepting His Son Jesus Christ as Savior and Lord.
>
> --Lenard A. Hartley

---

[3] Matthew 7:7-8, HCSB.

This comment from Len Hartley's questionnaire helps us put first things first. The foundation for a lifetime of helping ourselves to God's help is a personal relationship with Jesus Christ.

God does not violate our freedom to choose for ourselves whether or not we will trust in Jesus Christ for forgiveness and for the gift of eternal life.

> *The foundation for a lifetime of helping ourselves to God's help is a personal relationship with Jesus Christ.*

Jesus Christ died on a cross to make God's help available to us, but like the two men who died on crosses with Him, we make up our own minds about whether or not to put our faith in Him. One of the two thieves rejected Jesus Christ. But the other one helped himself to God's help by saying, "Jesus, remember me when you come into your Kingdom." And Jesus replied, "I assure you, today you will be with me in paradise."[4]

Why would anyone want to miss paradise by missing Jesus Christ?

When we put our faith in Jesus, we put ourselves in position to spend the rest of our lives helping ourselves to God's help. If you haven't yet put your faith in Christ, why not do so right now?

Accepting God's Will

> I need to abandon my will,
> continuously seeking His will.
>
> --Doris Bullock

---

[4] Luke 23:42-43, NLT.

> The Sovereign LORD has spoken to me,
> and I have listened. I do not rebel or turn away.
>
> --Isaiah 50:5, NLT

Sometimes we need for God to help us accept His help, and one way God helps us is by revealing His will to us. So we may even need to pray, "Lord, help me to accept Your help by helping me to accept Your will." Even asking for God's help won't work if we refuse the help that He offers us when He shows us His will.

> *We may even need to pray, "Lord, help me to accept Your help by helping me to accept Your will."*

So accepting God's help includes accepting Jesus Christ as our personal Lord and Savior. And accepting God's help also means accepting His will.

Of course, accepting Jesus Christ as our personal Lord and Savior is a good first step in accepting God's will, because the Bible says, "The Lord is not slow about His promise, as some count slowness, but is patient toward you, not wishing for any to perish but for all to come to repentance" (2 Peter 3:9, NASB). This Bible verse means that part of God's preferred will is that everyone on the planet would accept Jesus Christ as his or her personal Lord and Savior. God doesn't want anyone to perish.

Aspiring to Let God Help Me to Higher Ground

As we begin our journey of helping ourselves to God's help through faith in Jesus Christ, our dreams and aspirations will become increasingly spiritual or God-centered. And since God's ways are higher than our ways, we need to aim for higher ground.

> *Since God's ways are higher than our ways, we need to aim for higher ground.*

One way we can aim for higher ground is by . . .

Aspiring to Glorify God

> Give God the glory.
> It's all about Him.
>
> --Donna Riddle

If God didn't exist, neither would we. Since God created us, He has the right to determine the purposes of our lives. According to the Bible, our primary purpose is to glorify God. In the Book of Isaiah God says of His people, "for I have made them for my glory. It was I who created them."[5] God created us to help the world know how great He is so that others will want to help themselves to His help. To glorify God means that we exalt Him with both our lips and lives.

> *"Whatever you eat or drink or whatever you do, you must do all for the glory of God."*

Paul the Apostle aspired to glorify God and urged others to do the same. In a letter to the Christians living in Corinth he said, "Whatever

---

[5] Isaiah 43:7, NLT.

you eat or drink or whatever you do, you must do all for the glory of God."[6]

Another way we can aim for higher ground is by . . .

Aspiring to Please God

Do you want to please God? According to the Bible "it is impossible to please God without faith. Anyone who wants to come to Him must believe that there is a God and that He rewards those who sincerely seek Him."[7]

Faith enables us to please God and faith enables us to help ourselves to His help. People who truly want to please God will tend to trust Him, and people who trust Him are more likely to help themselves to His help.

I love the old hymn called "Living for Jesus."

> *Faith enables us to please God and faith enables us to help ourselves to His help.*

Consider the following words from that hymn as they show us someone who aspires to please God:

> Living for Jesus a life that is true,
> Striving to please him in all that I do,
> Yielding allegiance, glad-hearted and free,
> This is the pathway of blessing for me.[8]

---

[6] 1 Corinthians 10:31, NLT.

[7] Hebrews 11:6, NLT.

[8] "Living for Jesus," in *Baptist Hymnal*, ed. William J. Reynolds (Nashville, Tennessee: Broadman Press, 1975), 348.

Aspiring to Do God's Will

> I pray I will completely surrender my all
> to Him and be submissive to His will.
>
> --Colleen Heath

I spoke earlier in this chapter of accepting God's will, but helping ourselves to God's help means going beyond merely accepting His will to actually *wanting* to fulfill it. And aspiring to please God and to glorify Him includes wanting to do God's will God's way.

Doing God's will God's way means following the leadership of the Holy Spirit. As Paul wrote, "If we are living now by the Holy Spirit, let us follow the Holy Spirit's leading in every part of our lives."[9]

Absorbing and Assimilating God's Truth

> By reading and studying God's Word,
> by prayer, and listening to the Holy
> Spirit, I am helping myself to God's help.
>
> --Beta Little

One way we can help ourselves to God's help is by helping ourselves to His Word – the Bible. As I said earlier, God's Word works and God works through His Word. People who love and study the Bible prepare themselves to receive God's help for whatever problems and opportunities await them in the future.

---

[9] Galatians 5:25, NLT.

I recommend both personal Bible study and study in a small group setting such as Sunday school in a church. Hearing the Bible preached is another way to expose yourself to God's truths. While I prefer live preaching in a local church setting, some good preachers present God's Word on the radio and television. You may also benefit from listening to audio cassette tapes or CDs of the Bible.

Acting in Obedience to God's Commands and Guidance

> The one who has My commands and keeps them is the one who loves Me. And the one who loves Me will be loved by My Father. I also will love him and reveal Myself to him.
>
> --John 14:21, HCSB
>
> I must be willing, and when the Holy Spirit gives me direction, I must faithfully follow.
>
> --Beta Little

One of the best ways to help ourselves to God's help is to follow His instructions. In other words, we need to go beyond hearing His Word to actually doing what God tells us to do.[10] We need to help ourselves to God's help by praying, "Lord, help me to act on the truths You have shown me."

> *One of the best ways to help ourselves to God's help is to follow His instructions.*

---

[10] See James 1:22.

God expects us to help ourselves to His help by doing what He says, but consistently doing God's will requires strength from beyond ourselves. In his book, *Letting God Help You*, John A. Redhead declares:

> Yet it is impossible to do the will of God without the help of God, and it is good to know that both belong to biblical faith. Whenever you are willing to say with our Lord, "I am come not to do my own will, but the will of him that sent me," then you have every right to say also, "God is my refuge and strength!"[11]

Adjusting Our Attitudes

Have you ever heard anyone talk about the need for an attitude adjustment?

In his book, *Self-Talk: Key to Personnel Growth*, David Stoop explains, "The one thing, from a human perspective, that seems to make the difference between those who succeed and those who fail is attitude. No matter whom you are, attitude really is everything – it's what makes the difference in every aspect of life."[12]

Absorbing and assimilating God's truth will play a key role in the adjustment of our attitudes. And so will God's Spirit as we allow Him to produce in us the Christ-like qualities known as the fruit of the Spirit.[13]

---

[11] John A. Redhead, *Letting God Help You* (Nashville, Tennessee: Abingdon Press, 1957), 7.

[12] David Stoop, *Self-Talk: Key to Personal Growth* (Grand Rapids, Michigan: Fleming H. Revell, 2000), 10.

[13] See Galatians 5:22-23.

Associating with People Who Help Themselves to God's Help

> Associate with people whose lives
> reveal they are receiving God's help.
>
> --Lenard A. Hartley

> Seek the counsel of a godly person
> -- a man or woman of God.
>
> --Milton Tyler

As believers in the Lord Jesus Christ, we have acknowledged our need for God, but we also need each other. A man who did a lot of studying about human relationships, Guy Greenfield, once said:

> I was born in a social matrix, and I was created to live in a social environment where others are as important to my welfare and happiness as are food, water, air, and safety. There are those to whom I must say in all honesty, "I need you, and you need me." We need each other.[14]

Paul the Apostle referred to believers, who make up the church, as the body of Christ, and in so doing he stressed our need for one another. While explaining the relationship between the various parts, or members, of the body of Christ to other parts, he asserted, "So the eye, cannot say to the hand, 'I don't need you!' nor again the head to the feet, 'I don't need you!'"[15]

---

[14] Guy Greenfield, *We Need Each Other* (Grand Rapids, Michigan: Baker Hook House, 1987), 13.

[15] 1 Corinthians 12:21, HCSB.

So helping ourselves to God's help includes helping ourselves to God's people – the church. The Bible tells us that God wants His children to help one another. "Carry one another's burdens; in this way you will fulfill the law of Christ."[16]

> *Helping ourselves to God's help includes helping ourselves to God's people – the church.*

Our need for each other has a lot to do with the idea of helping ourselves to God's help because helping ourselves to God's help includes helping ourselves to God's people. Even Christians who cut themselves off from the community of faith reduce their access to the help that God offers them through other believers.

During the writing of this book, I faced some major crises in my life. Like many other believers in the Lord Jesus Christ, I felt tempted to withdraw from other believers by dropping out of church. For the many years that I served as a pastor of churches, I had seen many other people make that same mistake and thereby cut themselves off from God's help through His people, so I resisted that temptation. I even confided in a few other believers some of my worst stuff, and God has continued to help me through them. In tough times give God a chance to help you through His people.

At the beginning of this section of this chapter, I quoted Milton Tyler as saying, "Seek the counsel of a godly person -- a man or woman of God." One way we gain access to God's help is to

> *In tough times give God a chance to help you through His people.*

---

[16] Galatians 6:2, HCSB.

seek advice from people who love Jesus Christ. Why? Because if they truly love the Lord they also will love people for whom Christ died, and that includes you and me. And love means meeting needs, including our need for spiritual counsel or advice.

Even people who lived before our time can help us learn how to help ourselves to God's help. My friend, Lenard Hartley, has led churches in Texas for at least 53 years. And since that time he has mentored a group of pastors in San Angelo for over seven years. I found all of his responses to my questionnaire quite helpful. He urged me to read the biographies of dedicated Christians as a good way to help myself to God's help. That's good advice for me and it is good advice for you, too.

> *One way we gain access to God's help is to seek advice from people who love Jesus Christ.*

Will God's Help Make Me Happy?

> Happy is the one whose help is the
> God of Jacob, whose hope is in the
> Lord his God, the Maker of heaven and
> earth, the sea and everything in them.
>
> --Psalm 146:5-6, HCSB

Life, liberty, and the pursuit of happiness – I'm glad we have the freedom to *pursue* happiness, but that's not how to get it. Focus instead on pursuing God's will and God's ways and you'll experience a deep inner joy beyond the half-hearted happiness of most people.

Instead of asking, "Will God's help make me happy?" perhaps we should ask, "Can I be happy without God's help?" To some degree the answer to that question depends on what you mean by *happiness*.

> *Instead of asking, "Will God's help make me happy?" perhaps we should ask, "Can I be happy without God's help?"*

Happiness Defined

People hold many different ideas about what constitutes happiness. Some folks like to make a distinction between happiness and joy. Most people don't make that distinction. Instead, they use these terms interchangeably.

Either way, we need some sort of definition of genuine happiness as presented in the Bible. Through the years I've done many studies of the word **blessed** as used in the Bible, especially in the Beatitudes. The word for "blessed" in the Beatitudes in Matthew 5 could be translated with the word "happy." Instead of "*Blessed* are the poor in the spirit, ..." we could say, "*Happy* are the poor in spirit, ..." But I still haven't explained what **happy** means.

During a study of the Beatitudes I discovered the suggestion that to be blessed by God is to be smiled upon by God. In other words, true happiness consists of a deep inner joy that comes from knowing that God looks favorably upon us. This approach makes sense because Christian joy or happiness must enable believers to experience happiness even when faced with difficult circumstances. True happiness or joy results from knowing that God smiles at us even in the roughest of times.

> *True happiness or joy results from knowing that God smiles at us even in the roughest of times.*

Just think about it – would you rather have God smiling at you or frowning at you? That's not a hard question to answer, is it?

The Hope of Happiness

Everybody wants happiness, but many people lack the hope that they'll ever attain it. But the Bible says, "Happy is the one whose help is the God of Jacob, whose hope is in the Lord his God."[1] These words link

---

[1] Psalm 146:5a, HCSB.

the concepts of God's help and our happiness with the reality of hope – a hope found in God. You see, when we consistently help ourselves to God's help, we can experience both hope and happiness.

As Charles Swindoll says in his book, *Laugh Again*, "God is no distant deity but a constant reality, a very present help whenever needs occur. So? So live like it. And laugh like it! Paul did. While he lived, he drained every drop of joy out of every day that passed."[2]

> *When we consistently help ourselves to God's help, we can experience both hope and happiness.*

The How of Happiness

> We can learn about choices and
> how to make the ones that will
> give us hope and happiness.
>
> --Frank Minirth[3]

Helping ourselves to God's help is a matter of choice because God doesn't force us to seek His help. Choices play a major role in our happiness or lack of happiness. Bad choices produce negative results while good choices produce positive results.

---

[2] Charles R. Swindoll, *Laugh Again* (Dallas, Texas: Word Publishing, 1991), 27.

[3] Frank Minirth, *In Pursuit of Happiness* (Grand Rapids, Michigan: Fleming H. Revell, 2004), 11.

> *Helping ourselves to God's help includes making the right choices.*

Helping ourselves to God's help includes making the right choices. Let's consider some crucial choices that bring a smile to God's face and joy to our hearts.

Choose Jesus Christ as Your Lord and Savior

Surely you've notice by now that I keep coming back to the truth that a personal relationship with Jesus Christ serves as the foundation for a lifetime of helping ourselves to God's help. To find help put your faith in Jesus Christ and then follow Him. He will always lead you toward help and hope.

> *To find help put your faith in Jesus Christ and then follow Him. He will always lead you toward help and hope.*

Choose Forgiveness for Yourself and Others

> Oh, what joy for those whose
> rebellion is forgiven, whose
> sin is put out of sight! Yes, what
> joy for those whose record the
> Lord has cleared of sin, ...
>
> --Psalm 32:1, NLT

According to this verse, what does forgiveness do for us? It results in joy or happiness. When we help ourselves to God's help by choosing to accept His forgiveness, we let happiness into our lives.

Of course, God expects us to forgive others, also. Refusing to forgive others or yourself makes you a prisoner of the past.

What can we do to change the past? Absolutely nothing!

> *When we help ourselves to God's help by choosing to accept His forgiveness, we let happiness into our lives.*

Who does resentment hurt the most? Those who hold on to it. As Rick Warren explains in his book, *The Purpose Driven Life*, "Resentment always hurts you more than it does the person you resent."[4]

> Are you angry with your brother?
> Is there murder in your heart?
> If you let that anger stay there,
> you're surely not too smart.[5]

When we choose forgiveness for ourselves and for others, we help ourselves to happiness. So we all need to get forgiveness and then give it away. It makes absolutely no sense to accept forgiveness from God and then to refuse to give it to others. The Bible says, "Be kind to one another, tender-hearted, forgiving each other, just as God in Christ also has forgiven you."[6]

> *Get forgiveness and then give it away.*

---

[4] Rick Warren, *The Purpose Driven Life* (Grand Rapids, Michigan: Zondervan, 2002), 28.

[5] Travis Monday, "Before Sundown," in *Poems of Faith for People of Faith* (United States of America: Lulu Press, 2006), 5.

[6] Ephesians 4:32, NASB.

Choose to Rejoice in the Lord

> Rejoice in the Lord always.
> Again I will say, rejoice!
>
> --Philippians 4:4, NKJV

Paul urged the believers at Philippi to choose to rejoice in their relationship with the Lord Jesus Christ. Did you notice *when* we are to rejoice in the Lord? Always – "Rejoice in the Lord always." I don't know how anyone could possibly rejoice "always," that is, under all circumstances, without first helping themselves to God's help.

Choose to Focus Your Thoughts on Positive Realities

> Fix your thoughts on what is true, and honorable, and right, and pure, and lovely, and admirable. Think about things that are excellent and worthy of praise.
>
> --Philippians 4:8, NLT

These words from Paul the Apostle reveal his concern about the thought patterns of his fellow believers in the Lord Jesus Christ. Paul wanted them to intentionally and consistently think about positive realities rather than negative realities.

My pastor at Immanuel Baptist Church in San Angelo, Texas, Rev. James Mitchell, recently said something that fits well with Paul the Apostles' words in Philippians 4:8. He preached a series of messages on HOPE, and he let the letters of the word "HOPE" represent the following words: Having Only Positive Expectations.

So when you choose what you think about, choose wisely.

The Happiness of Heaven

> In My Father's house are many dwelling places; if it were not so, I would have told you; for I go to prepare a place for you."
>
> --John 14:2, NASB

When we help ourselves to God's help by putting our faith in Jesus Christ, we set the stage for eternal happiness in heaven. Everyone who trusts in Jesus Christ as Savior and Lord can expect to go to heaven to a place prepared for them by the Lord Jesus Himself. And do you know what makes heaven heavenly? The presence of God does!

> Have you ever thought of heaven –
> that grand and glorious place?
> Have you ever come to realize that
> to get there takes God's grace?
> Have you seen that it's the finish line
> for runners in God's race?
> Do you know that when we get there
> we'll look into Christ's face?[7]

And the Book of Revelation includes the following promise to followers of Jesus Christ: "He (God) shall wipe away every tear from their eyes; and

---

[7] Monday, "Heavenly Thoughts," in *Poems of Faith for People of Faith*, 24.

there shall no longer be *any* death; there shall no longer be *any* mourning, or crying, or pain."[8]

So, thanks to what God has done for us through His Son Jesus Christ, imperfect people like you and me can expect to enjoy forever heavenly happiness in a perfect place with our perfect God.

> *When we help ourselves to God's help by putting our faith in Jesus Christ, we set the stage for eternal happiness in heaven.*

---

[8] Revelation 21:4, NASB.

How Can I Help Others Get God's Help?

Somewhere along the line our focus on getting God's help for ourselves shifts to getting God's help for others. We discover that God has taken us from helplessness to helpfulness, and we find joy in helping others.

How can we help others gain access to God's help? Generally speaking, we learn how to help ourselves to God's help, and then we teach them what we've learned. We need to pray and ask God to send people to us and to send us to people whom we can teach what we've learned about helping ourselves to God's help.

Help Them Find Christ

People need Jesus Christ. If you really want to help people then help them to the Lord. Jesus can do more for others than you can.

> *People need Jesus Christ. If you really want to help people then help them to the Lord.*

Luke the Physician tells the following story of some men who overcame numerous obstacles in order to get their paralyzed friend to Jesus Christ:

> Now it happened on a certain day, as He was teaching, that there were Pharisees and teachers of the law sitting by, who had come out of every town of Galilee, Judea, and Jerusalem. And the power of the Lord was present to heal them.

> Then behold, men brought on a bed a man who was paralyzed, whom they sought to bring in and lay before Him. And when they could not find how they might bring him in, because of the crowd, they went up on the housetop and let him down with his bed through the tiling into the midst before Jesus.
>
> When He saw their faith, He said to him, "Man, your sins are forgiven you."[1]

The verses that follow indicate that Jesus healed the man of his paralysis so that he stood up and walked.

Why did the friends of this paralyzed man go to so much trouble to get him to Jesus? Because they believed that Jesus could help him. The best thing we can do for others is to get them to Jesus.

> Jesus Christ is all that's needed;
>
> Jesus Christ is still enough.
>
> He can heal the heart that's hurting;
>
> He can help when things get rough.[2]

Yes, these men wanted to get their friend to Jesus. And they did whatever it took to get him to the Lord.

> *The best thing we can do for others is to get them to Jesus.*

As I write this book, I'm serving the Lord as a hospital chaplain, so I have many opportunities to try to help others. Because my ministry is an interfaith ministry, I attempt to

---

[1] Luke 5:17-20, NKJV.

[2] Travis Monday, "Enough," in *Poems of Faith for People of Faith* (United States of America: Lulu Press, 2006), 5.

help people of many different religious traditions, including some that reject Jesus Christ. Although I treat everyone I visit with respect and do not attempt to force my beliefs on them, I always hope for an opportunity to exalt Jesus Christ in their presence. Why? Because I know that Jesus can help them more than I can.

> Reach out in faith to Jesus Christ,
>
> believing in your heart;
>
> His power will surge into your life;
>
> He'll give you a fresh start.
>
> Faith in Him will build you up
>
> while the world tries to tear you down.
>
> His grace is enough
>
> to put your feet
>
> on sure and solid ground.[3]

Help Them Follow Christ

After we find Jesus for ourselves we need to follow Him. When we consistently follow the Lord, we are helping ourselves to God's help. And when we teach others to follow Christ, we are teaching them how to help themselves to God's help.

Don't settle for just learning to follow Christ. Go beyond that to helping others follow Him also. In other words, make disciples by teaching them what you know about living for the Lord. Don't treat the

---

[3] Monday, "Power Source," in *Poems of Faith for People of Faith*, 3.

knowledge you gain from walking with Jesus as some sort of secret. The Lord wants you to share it.

> *When we teach others to follow Christ, we are teaching them how to help themselves to God's help.*

I want to see through Jesus' eyes

the people who surround me.

I want to love with Christ-like love

the sad, the sick, the hurting.

Lord, reach through me to someone else

before the day is through.

And as You do, I'll do my best

to praise and honor You.[4]

---

[4] Monday, "Perspective" in *Poems of Faith for People of Faith*, 14.

Can I Help God?

Helping God by Helping Myself to His Help

> O Jerusalem, Jerusalem, the city that kills
> the prophets and stones God's messengers!
> How often I have wanted to gather your
> children together as a hen protects her chicks
> beneath her wings, but you wouldn't let me.
>
> --Matthew 23:37, NLT

> Then Jesus said, "Come to me,
> all of you who are weary and carry
> heavy burdens, and I will give you rest."
>
> --Matthew 11:28, NLT

This reminder of our need to help ourselves to God's help is intended to keep us from getting the cart before the horse. In other words, helping God begins with letting Him help us. We start the process of helping God by first helping ourselves to His help. Until we trust in Jesus Christ enough to let Him become our Lord and Savior, we are in no position to become His servants.

> *Helping God begins with letting Him help us.*

God needs our help in order to help us. Why? Because He refuses to force His help upon us. In other words, I can help God fulfill His desire to help me. How? By *letting* Him help me.

Have you ever heard anyone say, "Let go and let God?" Well that's still a good concept and it helps us understand what it means to help ourselves to God's help.

One of the Best Things I've Learned

In order to help you better understand the concept of letting go and letting God, I want to share something with you that helps me. I do not know who to credit with this approach to getting God's help. Tim Sledge, a pastor in Katy, Texas, used it in a message I heard him preach. Later I found the same basic approach in an excellent book by Stephen Arterburn and Tim Timmons entitled, *Hooked On Life*. The version used by Arterburn and Timmons reads as follows:

>Step No. 1: "I Can't"
>
>Step No. 2: "God Can"
>
>Step No. 3: "I'll Let Him"[1]

The version used by Tim Sledge is essentially the same.

I've added a fourth component or step basically designed to reinforce the first three steps. Let's take a closer look at it. I start by saying . . .

1. *I Can't.*

I admit that I can't do something. I might say, "I admit that, in my own strength and abilities, I cannot produce the kind of fruit that God wants from me." Jesus said, "I am the vine, you are the branches; he who abides

---

[1] Tim Timmons and Stephen Arterburn, *Hooked On Life* (Nashville, Tennessee: 1989), 211-13.

in Me and I in him, he bears much fruit, for apart from Me you can do nothing."[2]

This statement goes along with what I said in earlier chapters about admitting our need for God's help. Until I'm ready to admit my need for Him, I cannot take advantage of the help the Lord offers.

> *After admitting that I can't do something, I shift the focus from me to the Lord.*

After admitting that I can't do something, I shift the focus from me to the Lord by saying . . .

2. God Can.

I *tell myself the truth* by saying that God can do what I cannot do. You see, God can handle anything we face no matter how bad it may seem. He is able to deliver us. He is able to help us.

After saying that I can't but God can, I then say . . .

> *God can handle anything we face no matter how bad it may seem. He is able to deliver us. He is able to help us.*

3. I'm Going to Let Him.

By *saying* that I am going to let God help me, I am verbalizing my *choice* to let God help me – an important choice since God does not force me to accept His help. And by *verbalizing* my choice, I help embed it in my consciousness.

In order to strengthen these first three steps I then say . . .

---

[2] John 15:5, NASB.

4. Therefore, I Can Do All Things Through Christ Who Strengthens Me.

Having made the choice to let God help me, I can then join Paul the Apostle in saying, "I can do all things through Him who strengthens me."[3]

I hope you can see that by taking myself through this process of *consciously choosing* to let the Lord help me, I am helping myself to Jesus, which is the essence of helping myself to God's help.

> *I can then join Paul the Apostle in saying, "I can do all things through Him who strengthens me."*

God's Invitation to Help Him

Helping myself to God's help means
knowing that God is always working and
that I have the privilege of being included.

--Donna Riddle

If anyone serves Me, let him
follow Me; and where I am,
there shall My servant also be;
if anyone serves Me, the
Father will honor him.
--John 12:26, NASB.

Jesus called out to them, "Come, be my disciples,
and I will show you how to fish for people!"
--Matthew 4:19, NLT

---

[3] Philippians 4:13, NASB.

When God invites us to salvation, He also invites us to service. In his book, *Letting God Help You*, John A. Redhead says, "Let God help you; yes, but that is only the beginning. More power to you is always more power *through* you."[4]

God invites us to help Him with His work.

Accepting God's Invitation

> I plead with you to give your bodies
> to God. Let them be a living and
> holy sacrifice – the kind he will accept.
>
> --Rom. 12:1a, NLT

While God doesn't need our help in order to survive and thrive, He definitely *wants* it. One of the reasons God wants our help is that He wants what's best for us, and the only way we can experience God's best is by learning to serve Him.

> *While God doesn't need our help in order to survive and thrive, He definitely wants it.*

When we talk about helping God, we're really just talking about serving Him, and the Bible clearly teaches us to serve Him. Joshua, one of the

---

[4] John A. Redhead, *Letting God Help You* (Nashville, Tennessee: Abingdon Press, 1957), 125.

early leaders of God's people, declared, "But as for me and my family, we will serve the LORD."[5]

Paul urged the believers in Rome to offer themselves to God as living sacrifices so that God could use them to accomplish His work in this world.

Do you want to help God? Then accept His invitation. Jesus said, "Follow Me, and I will make you . . . ." If we'll let Him, Jesus will make us – He will make us into whatever He wants us to be so that we can help Him with His work.

God can help us help Him. He also can help us keep on helping Him. As Redhead explains, "God never sends you on a trip without filling your tank with gas, and as long as you are committed to the King's business, your gas will hold out."[6]

Jesus said, "Follow Me, and I will make you fishers of men." Jesus invites us to help ourselves to His help, and His help includes teaching us how to help Him offer His help to others.

> *His help includes teaching us how to help Him offer His help to others.*

---

[5] Joshua 24:15, NLT.

[6] Redhead, 8.

Bibliography

Arterburn, Stephen, and Timmons, Tim. *Hooked On Life*. Nashville, Tennessee: Oliver Nelson Publishers, 1989.

Blackaby, Henry T. *Experiencing God*. Nashville, Tennessee: LifeWay Press, 1994.

Brown, H. C., Jr., *A Search for Strength*. Waco, Texas: Word Books, 1967.

Duncan, James E., Jr. *Relax and Let God* . . . Nashville, Tennessee: Broadman Press, 1975.

Greenfield, Guy. *We Need Each Other*. Grand Rapids, Michigan: Baker Book House, 1987.

Hastings, Robert J. *How to Help Yourself by Letting Him Help You*. Nashville, Tennessee: Broadman Press, 1981.

Hendrix, Richard. *Leadership*. Volume 7, Number 3.

Holmes, Marjorie. *To Help You Through the Hurting*. Garden City, New York: Doubleday & Company, Inc., 1983.

How to Let God Help You Through Hard Times. Lincolnwood, Illinois: Publications International, Ltd., 2001.

Lively, Bob. *God Help Me Through Today: Psalm 23 Revisited*. Harrisburg, Pennsylvania: Morehouse Publishing, 2001.

"Living for Jesus" in *Baptist Hymnal*, ed. William J. Reynolds. Nashville, Tennessee: Broadman Press, 1975.

May, Carl. *You Can Do It!* Nashville, Tennessee: Broadman Press, 1977.

Minirth, Frank. *In Pursuit of Happiness.* Grand Rapids, Michigan: Fleming H. Revell, 2004.

_____, and Meier, Paul D. *Happiness Is a Choice.* Grand Rapids, Michigan: Baker Book House, 1988.

Monday, Travis. *Basic Baptist Beliefs.* United States of America: Lulu Press, 2004.

_____. *Poems of Faith for People of Faith.* United States of America: Lulu Press, 2006.

Our Daily Bread. Ed. Tom Gustafon. Volume 51, Number 9, 10 & 11. December 2006, January & February 2007.

Parham, A. Philip. *Letting God: Christian Meditations for Recovering Persons.* San Francisco, California: Harper & Row, Publishers, 1987.

Redhead, John A. *Letting God Help You.* Nashville, Tennessee: Abingdon Press, 1957.

Speas, Ralph. *How to Deal with How You Feel.* Nashville, Tennessee: Broadman Press, 1980.

Stoop, David. *Self-Talk: Key to Personal Growth.* Grand Rapids, Michigan: Fleming H. Revell, 2000.

Swindoll, Charles R. *Laugh Again.* Dallas, Texas: Word Publishing, 1991.

Thomas A. Harris. *I'm Ok – You're OK.* New York: Avon Books, 1973.

Thorn, W. E. *Dairy Queen "Think Tank."* Fayetteville, North Carolina: Old Mountain Press, Inc., 2002.

Tiede, Tom. *Self-Help Nation.* New York: Atlantic Monthly Press, 2001.

Warren, Rick. *Purpose Driven Life.* Grand Rapids, Michigan: Zondervan, 2002.

West Texas Stockman, 1 July 1902. Page 1.

Wilbur, L. Perry. *How To Live Your Faith*. Englewood Cliffs, New Jersey: Prentice Hall, Inc., 1984.

Yancy, Philip. *Disappointment with God*. Grand Rapids, Michigan: Zondervan Publishing House, 1988.

www.ingramcontent.com/pod-product-compliance
Lightning Source LLC
Chambersburg PA
CBHW020019050426
42450CB00005B/557